Billy,
the Confused
Goat

ISBN 979-8-88540-089-3 (paperback)
ISBN 979-8-88540-090-9 (digital)

Christian Faith Publishing
832 Park Avenue
Meadville, PA 16335
www.christianfaithpublishing.com

Printed in the United States of America

Billy, the Confused Goat

JC LeDobree

There once was a happy old farmer. The farmer had a small home and many animals on his farm. On his farm, he had many cows and chickens, several ducks, and a few goats. Each group of animals was separated by their own groups.

The cows and goats were in the pasture, the chickens were in the coop, and the ducks had the pond. One day a young goat, named Billy looked around at the many cows of different colors. Black and white, black and brown, some were all black, and some were all brown. The young goat, Billy looked down at himself. Billy noticed that he was different from the cows. He was gray and white and shorter than the cows and left a smaller footprint, but yet he did the same as the cows.

Billy wanders the pastures, eats grass and hay, and beds with cows at night.

I feel like I should be a cow, Billy thought to himself. He decided to ask the farmer what he was.

Love God

"Farmer?" asked Billy. "What am I am?"

The farmer looked at him and said, "Why you're a goat."

Billy looked sad and replied, "But I feel like I'm a cow. I eat grass and hay, walk the pastures all day, and even bed in the barn with the cows."

"Well, "just because you feel like something else doesn't mean you are. Goats and cows are totally different animals," said the farmer. "You do very similar things throughout life, but you are completely different because of that which makes you a goat."

Billy walked away from the farmer with his head low.
"I'm going be to a cow because I feel I am one," said Billy.

So Billy decided to start changing his appearance to be more cowlike. One day Billy cut his long beard off. He walked out to the pasture and asked the farmer again.

"Farmer, what am I?"

"Why you're still a goat," replied the farmer.

"But I don't have a beard anymore," said Billy.

"Yes but you are still a goat because that's what God made you through your DNA, and God doesn't make mistakes," said the farmer.

Billy walked away upset. "It must be that I'm not colored correctly," said Billy. So that night, Billy colored himself solid black with white spots. The next morning, the farmer came to feed, and the goat approached him.

"What am I now, farmer?" Asked Billy.

"You're still a goat, my friend," replied the farmer.

"But I'm colored like a cow, I eat grass and hay, I bed with the cows in the barn at night, I have hoofs on my feet and no beard!" Billy expressed.

"Yes this is true goat," said the farmer. "But God created you to be a goat. The entire system that God gave you is made up of only that which makes you a goat."

Love God
WHITE
BLACK
BLACK

Billy walked away upset still. *It must be because I don't say moo,* he thought. Billy worked long and hard and finally learned to say *moo*. One day he walks to the farmer and starts saying *moo* as he feeds, in hopes that the farmer will notice him as a cow.

"Goat?" Asked the farmer. "How did you learn to say *moo*?"

"I'm not a goat," Billy replied. "I'm a cow."

"Unfortunately, goat, you're still a goat," replied the farmer.

"But I say *moo*, I eat grass and hay, I bed with cows, I no longer have a beard, I am no longer gray and white, I am black with white spots, I have hoofs on my feet, and I walk on all four legs," Billy replied. "How can I still be a goat? I feel I'm a cow. I look like a cow, so I am a cow," Billy expressed.

"Let's take a ride, Billy," replied the farmer.

The farmer loads Billy and one cow into his truck and trailer and drives them to a veterinarian.

"What are we doing here?" Billy asked. "We're not sick."

"No, goat, you're not sick," replied the farmer. "But I will show you why you're still a goat."

Love C

Billy, the cow, and the farmer go into the vet's office, and the vet draws a sample of blood from the goat and the cow, performs his test, and brings in the result for Billy and the farmer to see.

"See, Billy," said the vet. "Although you IDENTIFY as a cow, there's no denying that you're a goat through your DNA. The cow has a totally different strain in its blood than you," she finished.

The farmer took Billy and the cow back to his farm, and as he leads them to the pasture, he told Billy, "Now, as I said before, God made you a goat through that which makes you a goat and a cow through that which makes it a cow. No matter how much you change your outside appearance, you can NEVER become a cow," the farmer added, as he opens the gate to the pasture.

JUST BECAUSE ONE CAN IDENTIFY AND CHANGE THE OUTSIDE APPEARANCE OF THEMSELVES AS A DIFFERENT GENDER, IT DOES NOT CHANGE THAT WHICH MAKES YOU WHAT YOU ARE. THE DNA THAT GOD GAVE YOU CAN NEVER BE CHANGED, AND NO MATTER WHAT YOU SAY OR DO, GOD DOES NOT MAKE MISTAKES.

About the Author

Born in Indiana but grew up in South Central Kentucky his entire life, JC went straight to work out of high school and married his high school sweetheart, and twenty-four years later, they have three wonderful children, consisting of two girls and one boy, ranging in ages from twenty to eleven years old. JC discovered, at an early age, he had a passion for writing. As a child and a young adult, he was always writing short stories and jotting down ideas for other stories.

However, he had never written a children-themed story; his passion was more on horror and thriller stories. It wasn't until 2020 when he rededicated his life to Jesus Christ and that during a conversation with his father, God told him it was time to turn his God-given ability of writing into work for our Lord and Savior. JC's hopes are to do the work for our Lord and to bring people closer to God, especially children who are facing a very difficult time in this day and age.